ASIAN DEVELOPMENT BANK

SUSTAINABILITY REPORT 2020
PART I: HIGHLIGHTS

DECEMBER 2020

ASIAN DEVELOPMENT BANK

ASIAN DEVELOPMENT BANK

SUSTAINABILITY REPORT 2020
PART I: HIGHLIGHTS

DECEMBER 2020

ASIAN DEVELOPMENT BANK

ADB

CONTENTS

TABLES AND FIGURES

Tables

Figures

THE PRESIDENT'S STATEMENT

The Asian Development Bank (ADB) has long supported environmental, social, and financial sustainability in its operations and institutional practices. It makes me proud to lead an institution that continues to strive to "walk the sustainability talk" in its project investments, technical assistance services, and corporate footprint.

I am, therefore, very pleased to share this summary of ADB's sustainability highlights and its accompanying Global Reporting Initiative (GRI) Content Index, which presents the significant economic, social, and environmental impacts of ADB's operations and facilities for 2018 and 2019.

We release this report at a highly unusual and challenging time, when all 68 members of ADB in Asia and the Pacific, North America, and Europe are still reeling from the coronavirus disease (COVID-19) pandemic that has hobbled the global economy and fundamentally changed our way of life. The pandemic has revealed just how dependent human health and social and economic well-being are on the health of the environment and natural ecosystems.

Now, more than ever, it is critical that institutions like ADB are transparent about the sustainability of our operations and project financing as we look to jump-start a resilient, inclusive, and sustainable recovery for the region.

In 2018, in what was probably the most significant step toward embedding sustainability in ADB, we transitioned to a new long-term strategy—Strategy 2030—taking a more holistic approach to the region's changing needs, and offering a new road map for ADB to better respond to the diversity and aspirations of our developing member countries (DMCs).

ADB's Board of Directors then endorsed in October 2019 seven operational plans covering each of the seven priorities of Strategy 2030. These are designed to reinforce and complement one another, focusing on addressing remaining poverty and reducing inequalities; accelerating progress in gender equality; tacking climate change, building climate and disaster resilience, and enhancing environmental sustainability; making cities more livable; promoting rural development and food security; strengthening governance and institutional capacity; and fostering regional cooperation and integration. This summary report includes examples of some notable projects and initiatives that embody these priorities.

As a key monitoring mechanism, we approved in August 2019 a new Corporate Results Framework for 2019–2024. This is to ensure that ADB's actions and investments align with Strategy 2030 and our new operational priorities. The Corporate Results Framework includes key targets presented in Strategy 2030, including $80 billion in cumulative climate financing by 2030, with 75% of our total number of operations focusing on climate change mitigation and adaptation.

While we still have a long way to go to meet the ambitions set out in Strategy 2030, we are making progress as we continue to increase our efforts. Over the past 2 years, we expanded our support for environmentally sustainable, low-carbon, and resilient investments, with $4.54 billion in financing in 2018, followed by a record $6.56 billion in climate change investments in 2019. Such investments contributed to tangible outcome for sustainable development in our DMCs. For example, ADB's $2.4 billion investments in clean energy projects over 2018 and 2019 are expected to generate 4.6 gigawatts of additional capacity from renewable energy sources and 5.1 terawatt-hours in electricity savings, while cutting about 17.4 million tons of carbon dioxide emissions per year. The past 2 years also saw almost 1 million households provided with new and improved energy access.

ADB also views mobilizing resources from the private sector as critical to ensure sustainable development. Financing from ADB for two landmark, first-ever green bonds issuances by our clients is a case in point, with financing in 2019 for the AC Energy Green Bond Project ($20 million) and the Energy Absolute Green Bond for Wind Power Project ($98.2 million, or ฿3 billion). Another good example is the ASEAN Catalytic Green Finance Facility that ADB launched in April 2019 with with Association of Southeast Asian Nations (ASEAN) countries and development partners. The facility aims to spur more than $1 billion in green and climate-friendly infrastructure investments, such as sustainable transport, clean energy, and resilient water systems across Southeast Asia by mobilizing investments from the private sector.

In May 2019, we launched an Action Plan for Healthy Oceans and Sustainable Blue Economies, committing to scale-up investments and technical assistance for ocean health between 2019 and 2024. The plan prioritizes protecting and restoring coastal and marine ecosystems and key rivers, reducing land-based sources of marine pollution, including plastics, and improving the sustainability of coastal infrastructure development.

We also increased our support to improve social inclusion and services to the most vulnerable and marginalized communities. We are committed to delivering gender equality results in at least 80% of completed projects by 2024, having already achieved a 3-year average of 74% of projects during the 2017–2019 period.

We launched thematic bonds that enable socially responsible investors to fund projects, with bonds issued for gender ($46.9 million in 2018 and $51.5 million in 2019), water ($12.3 million in 2018) and health ($12.8 million in 2019). This is in addition to the $1.76 billion for green bonds issued in 2018 and $2.59 billion issued in 2019, which included an Australian $1 billion Kangaroo green bond, the largest Supranational, Sovereign and Agency (SSA) Kangaroo green bond at the time of issuance in 2019.

At the institutional level, we continue to take actions to improve our corporate footprint and resource management. In addition to using renewable energy to power our headquarters, we encourage the use of videoconferencing to reduce air travel and use green vehicles when possible. We remain carbon neutral through the purchase of carbon credits for residual emissions. Our headquarters in Manila was recertified to International Organization for Standardization (ISO) 14001, 45001, and 50001 in 2018. Since 2011, we have maintained gold certification in Leadership in Energy and Environmental Design (LEED) practices and specification for operating and maintaining green buildings.

As part of the Human Resources Framework for diversity and mutual respect among staff, we established the Office of Professional Conduct in 2019 to better address workplace concerns. Women comprised 36% of all international staff in 2018 and 37% in 2019, putting us on track to meet our transitional target of 38% by 2020, as we progress toward our longer-term corporate target of 40% by 2022. I am also proud to share that in 2019, ADB marked the International Day Against Homophobia, Transphobia, and Biphobia (IDAHOT) by hosting events over 2 days at ADB headquarters in Manila and also became the first international financial institution to earn the second tier EDGE (Economic Dividends for Gender Equality) Move Certification, demonstrating significant progress in ADB's gender representation, pay equity, effectiveness of policies, and practices to ensure equitable career flows and inclusiveness.

We have updated our Public Communications Policy into an expanded Access to Information Policy to further enhance transparency of our operations and internal management. We are also currently re-evaluating our key policies on energy, and environmental and social safeguards, and improving how we measure our impact and evaluate our results. These actions will ensure that our efforts remain effective, efficient, and sustainable; and member countries and stakeholders are better informed about our operations and results.

As Asia and the Pacific recovers from the impact of COVID-19, ADB is listening carefully and responding to the urgent needs of our DMCs. Let me also make it clear that even during the extraordinary period of the pandemic, ADB has not wavered from the ambitious targets set by Strategy 2030 on critical issues such as climate change and gender. Building back better through a green, inclusive, resilient, and sustainable recovery will be critical for the region's future and ADB stands ready to support.

We hope you enjoy reading this summary report and the accompanying GRI Contents Index.

MASATSUGU ASAKAWA

President and Chairperson of the Board of Directors
Asian Development Bank

ACKNOWLEDGMENTS

Preparation of the Sustainability Report was overseen by Woochong Um, director general, Sustainable Development and Climate Change Department (SDCC); and Lakshmi Menon, principal director, Office of Administrative Services; and led by Bruce Dunn, director of the Safeguards Division, SDCC and concurrently officer-in-charge of the Environment Thematic Group.

Preparation and production of this summary report was managed by Duncan Lang, senior environment specialist, SDCC with core support from Marie Antoinette Virtucio, Cristina R. Velez (consultant), Ross Locsin Laccay (consultant), Christopher Darius M. Tabungar, as well as Phil Hughes (consultant), who provided technical guidance. In addition, essential support was also provided by Erwin R. Casaclang, facilities planning and management officer, Office of Administrative Services; and Bianca Nela D. De la Isla, senior operations assistant, Budget, Personnel, and Management Systems Department. Karen Williams (consultant), and Monina Gamboa copyedited this report for publication.

The following focal points provided essential information and advice:

Christel Adamou, Wilfredo Agliam, Meenakshi Ajmera, Angelica Alejandro, Michelle Apostol, Agnes Kristine Arban, Md. Abul Basher, Julia Cummins, Erwin Casaclang, Mary Jane Carangal-San Jose, Alexandra Pamela Chiang, Olimpia Henriques da Silva, Irene Dionisio, Lydia Domingo, Roqueña Domingo, Minhong Fan, Coral P. Fernandez-Illescas, Sanjay Grover, Sharad Ghosh, Dorothy C. Geronimo, Amal Hakki, Tadateru Hayashi, Andrew Head, Neil Hickey, Arndt Husar, Esmyra Javier, Thomas Kessler, Jamie Kho, Pei Ling Koh, Hazel Lalas, Catherine Leonillo, Cai Li, Jeffrey Liang, Cholpon Mambetova, Rie Matsubayashi, Duncan Mcleod, Josefina Miranda, Mark Morales, Antoine Morel, Takako Morita, Kee-Yung Nam, Smita Nakhooda, Keiko Nowacka, Arlene Pantua, Rishmil Patel, Aldrin Plaza, Przemek Prutis, Mailene Radstake, Vivek Raman, Mirko Rizzuto, Amuerfina Santos, Srinivas Sampath, Malika Shagazatova, Rajeev Singh, Charity Torregosa, Tomoo Ueda, Orlee Velarde, Carmela Villamar, and Jean Williams

We also gratefully received assistance from many people across ADB, including Leah Arboleda, Marissa L. Barcenas, Haidy Seang Ear-Dupuy, Metis Ilagan, Christopher I. Morris, Wilhelmina T. Paz, Nissanka Amila Buddika Salgado, Elaine Thomas, and Michelle Tumilba.

ABBREVIATIONS

ADB	Asian Development Bank
ADF	Asian Development Fund
AML/CFT	Anti-Money Laundering/Combating the Financing of Terrorism
ASEAN	Association of Southeast Asian Nations
CAREC	Central Asia Regional Economic Cooperation
DMC	developing member country
E2HSMS	Energy, Environment, Health, and Safety Management System
EDGE	Economic Dividends for Gender Equality
GHG	greenhouse gas
GMS	Greater Mekong Subregion
GRI	Global Reporting Initiative
ISO	International Organization for Standardization
Lao PDR	Lao People's Democratic Republic
LEED	Leadership in Energy and Environmental Design
LPG	liquefied petroleum gas
LPR	law and policy reform
MDB	multilateral development bank
NDC	nationally determined contribution
OHSAS	Occupational Health and Safety Assessment Series
OP	operational priority
PRC	People's Republic of China
SDG	Sustainable Development Goal
SOE	state-owned enterprise
SPADE	Spatial Data Analysis Explorer
SPS	Safeguard Policy Statement
TA	technical assistance

I. SUSTAINABILITY HIGHLIGHTS, 2018–2019

Launched Strategy 2030—closely aligned with Sustainable Development Goals (SDGs) and the Financing for Development Agenda, the Paris Agreement on climate change, the Sendai Framework for Disaster Risk Reduction, and the G20 agenda for quality infrastructure (2018)—and mainstreamed the Seven Operational Priorities (2019).

Energy, environment, health, and safety management system **recertified to the International Organization for Standardization (ISOs) 14001, 45001, and 50001 in 2018**.

Since 2011, maintained Gold certification in Leadership in Energy and Environmental Design (LEED) for operating and maintaining green buildings.

In 2019, ADB became the first international financial institution (IFI) to voluntarily achieve the second level of Economic Dividends for Gender Equality

Surpassed $6 billion climate commitments in 2019, 1 year ahead of schedule

In 2019, ADB set a record high of $6.55 billion in climate-related financing, meeting a key commitment to double its annual climate investments from $3 billion in 2014 to $6 billion in 2020.

Action Plan for Healthy Oceans and Sustainable Blue Economies launched to scale-up investments and technical assistance in ocean $5 billion between 2019 and 2024

Three Main Focus Areas of Action Plan

Pollution control

Ecosystem and natural resource management

Sustainable development and infrastructure

Outcomes of ADB's clean energy and energy access investments

		2018	2019
Clean energy investment total		$1.4 billion	$1.0 billion
Renewable energy		$0.8 billion	$0.7 billion
Energy efficiency		$0.6 billion	$0.3 billion
Additional installed capacity using renewable energy gigawatt		0.6	4.0
Carbon dioxide (CO_2) reduction (million tons of CO_2 equivalent per year)		10.7	6.7
New and improved energy access (number of household, in thousands)		474.0	504.0

Greenhouse gas reduction from project investments

2018
2,431,000 tons
CO_2 equivalent

2019
12,778,000 tons
CO_2 equivalent

In 2019, ADB issued thematic bonds and green bonds totaling to **$2.7 billion** in Australian dollars, euros, Hong Kong dollars, Norwegian krone, pounds sterling, and Swedish krona.

Total outstanding green bonds at year-end

2018
$5 billion

2019
$6.8 billion

Outstanding thematic bonds totaled

water
$102 million

gender
$189 million

health
$110 million

2018 $430 million   2019 $401 million

II. ABOUT THE ASIAN DEVELOPMENT BANK

ADB is a multilateral development bank (MDB) established in 1966 whose purpose is to foster economic growth and cooperation in the Asia and Pacific region and to contribute to the economic development of its developing member countries (DMCs). ADB transfers resources from global capital markets to its DMCs through government (i.e., public sector or sovereign) and private sector (nonsovereign) projects.

ADB provides a range of financial products for the public and the private sectors, including loans, grants, and technical assistance (TA) from its special funds, including the Asian Development Fund; administers financing partnership facilities, trust funds, and other funds; promotes innovation; and disseminates knowledge and information, consistent with Strategy 2030.

By the end of 2019, ADB's total assets were $222 billion.

ADB is owned and governed by its 68 members

Capital provided by:

36.6% Europe and North America (19 nonregional members)

63.4% Asia and the Pacific (49 regional members)

The membership of ADB reflects the intention of its founders to limit its operations to the Asia and Pacific region, and also to incorporate the active participation and financial resources of members outside the region. At the end of 2019, the value of ADB's subscribed capital was $147.1 billion. Total shareholders' equity was $51.9 billion.

The overarching vision of ADB's long-term corporate strategy has been set out through Strategy 2030, which aims to achieve a prosperous, inclusive, resilient, and sustainable Asia and the Pacific, while sustaining efforts to eradicate extreme poverty. Strategy 2030 sets seven operational priorities, each with its own operational plan.

ADB invests in projects that create economic and development impact, supporting its DMCs' to reduce poverty and improve the quality of life of their people. Thus, ADB's beneficiaries are its DMCs and, ultimately, those people who benefit from improved living conditions and quality of life in these countries.

Solar panels installed at Asian Development Bank headquarters in Mandaluyong City, Metro Manila, Philippines. The panels provide clean, renewable energy to ADB headquarters as part of ongoing efforts to "walk the sustainability talk" and lead by example.

III. GOVERNANCE

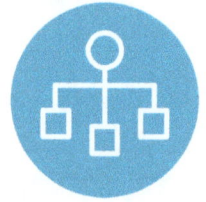

ADB's governance structure consists of a Board of Governors, a Board of Directors, the President, and the management team.

ADB's shareholders are represented on the Board of Governors, which serves without renumeration from ADB. Each DMC appoints a governor and an alternate governor (usually the DMC's minister of finance, central bank governor, or an official of similar rank), who serve at the member's pleasure. The Board of Governors meets once a year, at ADB's Annual Meeting, to provide guidance on ADB administrative, financial, and operational directions.

Figure 1: Functional Organization Chart, May 2020

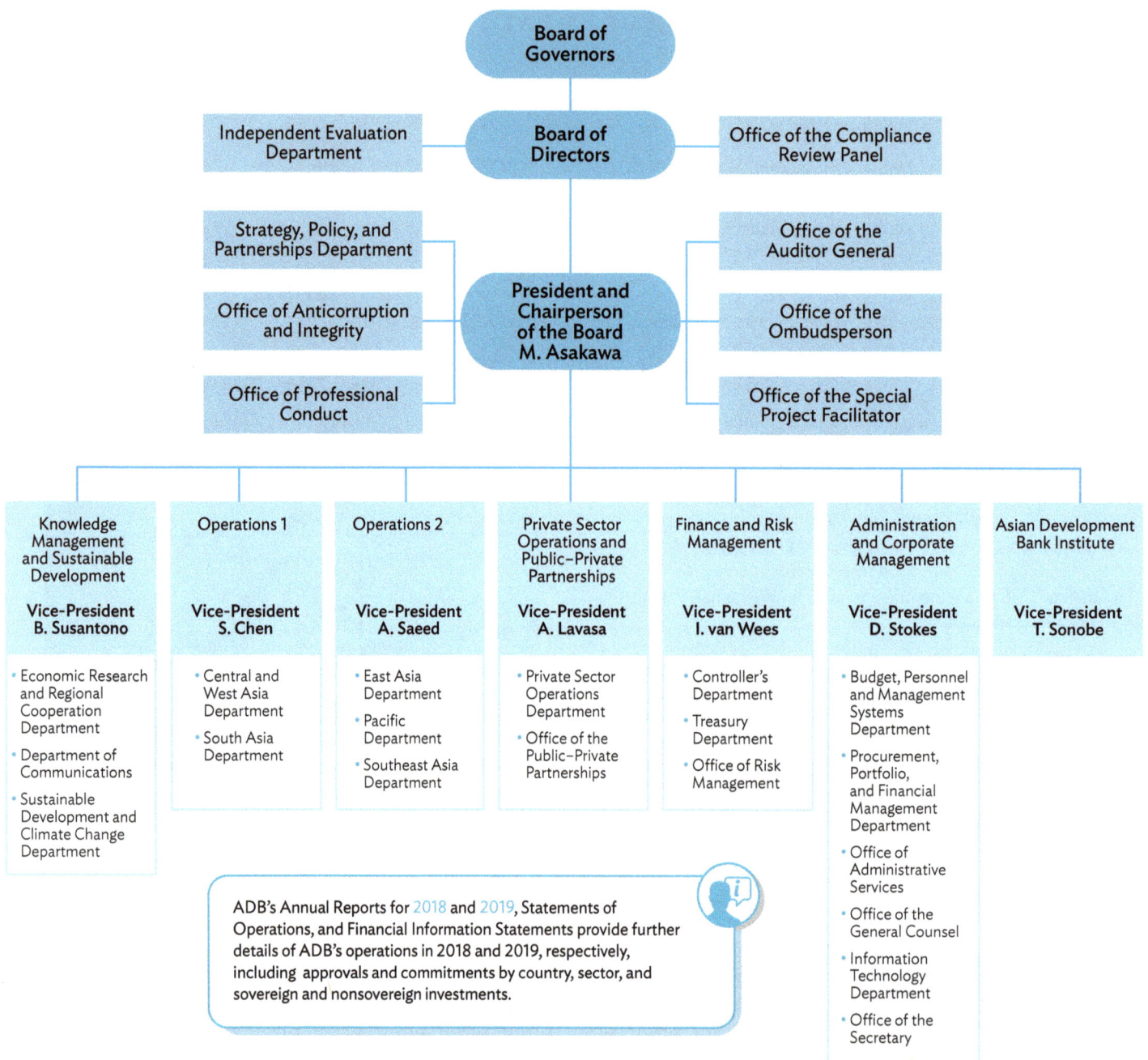

```
                        Board of
                        Governors
                            |
Independent Evaluation    Board of     Office of the Compliance
     Department          Directors           Review Panel
                            |
Strategy, Policy, and                   Office of the
Partnerships Department                 Auditor General

Office of Anticorruption  President and  Office of the
    and Integrity         Chairperson    Ombudsperson
                          of the Board
Office of Professional    M. Asakawa     Office of the Special
      Conduct                            Project Facilitator
```

Knowledge Management and Sustainable Development	Operations 1	Operations 2	Private Sector Operations and Public–Private Partnerships	Finance and Risk Management	Administration and Corporate Management	Asian Development Bank Institute
Vice-President B. Susantono	Vice-President S. Chen	Vice-President A. Saeed	Vice-President A. Lavasa	Vice-President I. van Wees	Vice-President D. Stokes	Vice-President T. Sonobe
• Economic Research and Regional Cooperation Department • Department of Communications • Sustainable Development and Climate Change Department	• Central and West Asia Department • South Asia Department	• East Asia Department • Pacific Department • Southeast Asia Department	• Private Sector Operations Department • Office of the Public–Private Partnerships	• Controller's Department • Treasury Department • Office of Risk Management	• Budget, Personnel and Management Systems Department • Procurement, Portfolio, and Financial Management Department • Office of Administrative Services • Office of the General Counsel • Information Technology Department • Office of the Secretary	

ADB's Annual Reports for 2018 and 2019, Statements of Operations, and Financial Information Statements provide further details of ADB's operations in 2018 and 2019, respectively, including approvals and commitments by country, sector, and sovereign and nonsovereign investments.

IV. ACCOUNTABILITY AND TRANSPARENCY

ADB retained its first place ranking in the 2020 Aid Transparency Index, an independent measure of aid transparency among the world's major development and aid organizations.

In 2018, the ADB Board of Directors approved a new Access to Information Policy that aims to maintain ADB's high standards of transparency. The new policy includes a new overarching principle of "clear, timely, and appropriate disclosure" that is underpinned by a presumption that favors disclosure and a commitment to sharing information and ideas. Under the new policy, ADB has expanded some areas of disclosure (e.g., the types of information that will be made available after 20 years) to include historical country financial information and certain external audit reports on ADB-administered trust funds.

ADB's Accountability Mechanism provides a forum for people adversely affected by ADB projects to voice their problems, seek solutions, and report alleged noncompliance with ADB's operational policies and procedures. This last-resort mechanism has two separate but complementary functions: problem-solving and compliance review. Under the Accountability Mechanism, operations departments are responsible for resolving the concerns of project-affected persons in the first instance and also for resolving issues pertaining to negative impacts from projects where ADB may be at fault.

In addition, and in line with ADB's Safeguard Policy Statement, consultation and information disclosure on environmental and social impacts from projects continues during implementation, as set out in safeguards plans. A project-level grievance redress mechanism is established to enable affected persons to raise their concerns with the borrower (client) and seek resolution.

ADB's website adb.org, is among the most important tools for sharing knowledge about ADB's activities and publishing the impacts of its operations.

In 2018, ADB received 4,043 official requests for documents; 71% received responses within 20 days. In 2019, the bank received 4,209 formal requests for information. Of these, 3,544 (84%) were deemed valid and the rest were identified as spam. ADB acknowledged 69% of the valid requests within the required 7 days and responded to 83% within the required 30 days, thereby responding to 93% of valid requests by the end of the year.

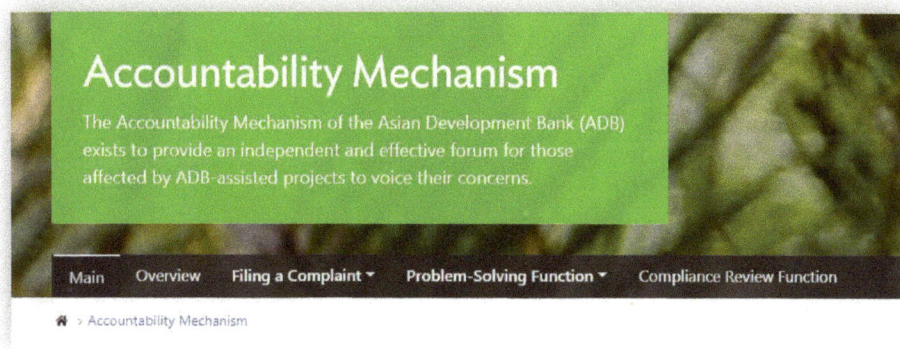

Accountability Mechanism

The Accountability Mechanism of the Asian Development Bank (ADB) exists to provide an independent and effective forum for those affected by ADB-assisted projects to voice their concerns.

Main   Overview   Filing a Complaint ▾   Problem-Solving Function ▾   Compliance Review Function

⌂ > Accountability Mechanism

V. STAKEHOLDER ENGAGEMENT

ADB consults and collaborates with a wide range of stakeholders, from governments to individuals, during the development, review, and evaluation of its safeguard, sector, and thematic policies and strategies and country partnership strategies; during project preparation, implementation, and evaluation; and through the economic, environmental, and social initiatives it undertakes in relation to its operations and organizational activities.

ADB also conducts stakeholder mapping and engagement in fragile and conflict-affected situations and countries to improve understanding of the context and improve project design and implementation, resulting in more sustainable projects in some of the most difficult environments ADB operates in.

Engaging with our stakeholders is vital to ensure that our policies reflect international best practice and incorporate the opinions and needs of those they intend to support. The participation process builds understanding and ownership of the policies and eases implementation. ADB papers that have been prepared with extensive consultations with stakeholders (including civil society organizations) include the

- Accountability Mechanism Policy,
- Public Communications Policy, and
- Safeguard Policy Statement summary of stakeholder consultations.

ADB also engages with its stakeholders (i.e., government officials; private sector; academe; students; media; journalists; civil society; the local community of the host country; providers of goods, works, and services; international organizations; development institutions; think tanks; multilateral development banks; international financial institutions; and others) during each annual meeting , whether by direct participation, social media, or involvement in its planning and organization. Each year, the profile of accredited stakeholders changes, depending on the meeting's location. Additionally, ADB regularly uses regional and national conferences and other events to share knowledge products and exchange views with government officials and other key audiences.

The annual meeting is a certified carbon-neutral event that follows internationally recognized principles for sustainable events. The Event Sustainability Team in the Office of the Secretary developed a how-to video (i.e., "Making Meetings Green and Sustainable"), and a related brochure and checklist, to share best practices with the host country on incorporating sustainability principles in all meetings and events. They work in tandem with the host country to integrate sustainable practices among suppliers and event organizers and develop activities promoting sustainability for all participants.

52nd ADB Annual Meeting: Host Country Seminar – 30 Under 30: The Faces of Fiji's Future. 2 May 2019. Host country seminar "30 Under 30: The Faces of Fiji's Future" at the 52nd Annual Meeting of the ADB Board of Governors. Panelists were selected from the inaugural class of "30 Under 30," a new initiative led by the Government of Fiji which solicited a truly talented pool of nominees.

VI. STRATEGY 2030: SEVEN OPERATIONAL PRIORITIES

The overarching vision of ADB's long-term corporate strategy (i.e., Strategy 2030) is to achieve a prosperous, inclusive, resilient, and sustainable Asia and the Pacific, while sustaining efforts to eradicate extreme poverty. Strategy 2030 sets Seven operational priorities (OPs), each with its own operational plan:

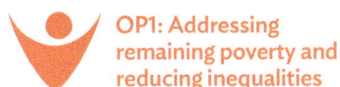

OP1: Addressing remaining poverty and reducing inequalities

OP4: Making cities more livable

OP7: Fostering regional cooperation and integration

OP2: Accelerating progress in gender equality

OP5: Promoting rural development and food security

OP3: Tackling climate change, building climate and disaster resilience, and enhancing environmental sustainability

OP6: Strengthening governance and institutional capacity

ADB is mobilizing public and private finance, strengthening knowledge services, and convening effective partnerships to proactively respond to the changing needs of the Asia and Pacific region.

In the following pages, we highlight some key ADB initiatives that embody and illustrate our operational priorities and differentiated approaches to address diverse client needs.

These projects and long-term programmatic initiatives are designed to deliver integrated yet customized solutions across a range of sectors and themes.

HOW ADB ADDS VALUE

FINANCE
Providing own financing while also mobilizing funds from other sources

KNOWLEDGE
Focusing on practical value that fits local conditions, identifies lessons, and replicates good practices

PARTNERSHIPS
Promoting dialogue and collaboration among diverse partners and stakeholders

PRINCIPLES THAT GUIDE US

USING COUNTRY-FOCUSED APPROACH
Providing customized solutions to each developing member country's (DMC's) specific development needs and challenges

PROMOTING THE USE OF INNOVATIVE TECHNOLOGY
Proactively seeking ways to use advanced technologies across operations and providing capacity building support to DMCs

DELIVERING INTEGRATED SOLUTIONS
Combining expertise across a range of sectors and themes, and through a mix of public and private sector operations

From top:

Children residing near the heating plant site in Selbe subcenter. The Ulaanbaatar Urban Services and Ger Areas Development Investment Program introduces sustainable urban services and supports the socioeconomic development of urban communities in subcenters located in ger areas.

Domestic Maritime Support (Sector) Project in Solomon Islands. People arriving from an inter island boat trip at the Port of Honiara.

Kazakh students playing the dombra. The dombra is a popular folk instrument in Kazakhstan.

Second Education Quality Improvement Project in the Lao PDR. Children enjoying school at the Ban Palai elementary school in Paklai District, Sayaboury Province.

From top:

Rural Primary Health Services Delivery Project. Preparing the Health Services Sector Development Program in Papua New Guinea. Villagers visit the Tsinjipai Community Health Post for information and treatments.

Making Dreams Come True in the Philippines with the Secondary Education Support Program. ADB's Secondary Education Support program is preparing students in the Philippines with job-ready skills

Sustainable Natural Resource Management and Productivity Enhancement Project in the Lao PDR. Farmers chopping cassava plants on a property in Lao Ngam District, Saravane Province, which received support under the Sustainable Natural Resource Management and Productivity Enhancement Project.

Majhi Metro 2016 Festival. One Day in Mumbai's Metro, Dreams (photo: Coralie Marcadé / ig: @digitalecoco).

From top:

Energy Conservation and Emissions Reduction from Poor Household in Mongolia. Ger is a round tent that serves as home to Mongolians with a nomadic lifestyle. The Energy Conservation and Emissions Reduction from Poor Household Project aims to improve the quality of life in ger housing areas.

Karnataka Urban Development and Coastal Environmental Management Project in India. Installation of low-cost toilets under the Karnataka Urban Development and Coastal Environmental Management Project in India.

Students in Bhutan. Students take time off their school activity to pose for the camera in Bhutan.

Improving Market Access for the Poor in Central Cambodia. This handicraft producer group is a beneficiary of an ADB-supported project to improve livelihoods by creating jobs for local people in Kampong Thom, Cambodia.

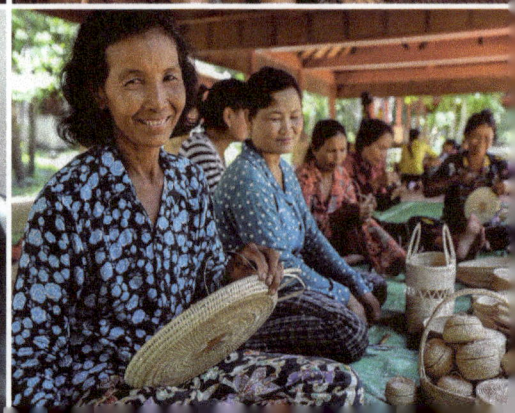

Operational Priority 1: Addressing Remaining Poverty and Reducing Inequalities

Human development and social inclusion, quality jobs, education and training, better health, social protection

Strategic Operational Priorities

1 Human capital and social protection enhanced for all

2 Quality jobs generated

3 Opportunities for the most vulnerable increased

Operational Approaches

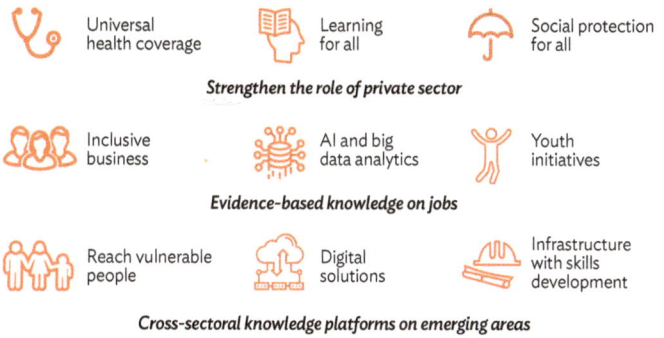

Universal health coverage

Learning for all

Social protection for all

Strengthen the role of private sector

Inclusive business

AI and big data analytics

Youth initiatives

Evidence-based knowledge on jobs

Reach vulnerable people

Digital solutions

Infrastructure with skills development

Cross-sectoral knowledge platforms on emerging areas

AI = artificial intelligence.

Philippines: Elevating Education and Employability of Millions of Students and Out-of-School Youth

Despite gains in enrollment and graduations since the 1990s, the secondary education system in the Philippines faces limited access and low-quality learning. Poor employee performance, particularly among 15–24-year-olds entering the job market for the first time, has also become a dominant problem in the labor market. These issues continue to drive an unrelenting cycle of poverty. To arrest the deterioration, two ADB projects support the government's education and labor reforms. ADB is helping elevate the quality and access to public secondary school education so that more students can compete effectively in the job market. So far, 1.3 million students have benefited from more classrooms, a new senior high school curriculum that includes a technical–vocational–livelihood track, along with a school voucher program. To reduce the number of out-of-school youth, ADB is improving their employability through labor market programs and access to on-the-job training schemes to help them secure and retain jobs. The program builds on ADB's collaboration with the Department of Labor and Employment through Jobstart Philippines, a full-cycle youth employment facilitation program that has become law with adequate government funding. Jobstart has rolled out in 35 local government units, benefiting 17,537 out-of-school youth.

Loan, Secondary Education Support Program: **$300 million**

Loan, Facilitating Youth School-To-Work Transition Program: **$400 million**

Papua New Guinea: Strengthening Health through Digital Health Systems

In Papua New Guinea, around 85% of the population lives in rural, often remote, areas, making it challenging to access quality health care. This is why, despite its economic rise in recent years, Papua New Guinea continues to have the highest maternal mortality ratios and infant mortality rates and lowest life expectancy among Pacific island countries. ADB is boosting government efforts in achieving universal health coverage to support the delivery of accessible, affordable, and high-quality health services. The intervention is enabling an integrated public health model that links primary and secondary health facilities in rural areas, supports decentralized health service delivery, and trains health-care staff in public financial management and reporting to better plan and budget. The bank is also rehabilitating rural health-care infrastructure, improving the availability of medical supplies, and supporting new health partnerships and the creation of digital information systems.

Loan: **$195 million**

Indonesia and Fiji: Revitalizing Informal Settlements Using a Water-Sensitive Approach

Unplanned growth, urban sprawl, and governments' incapacity to improve upon sustainable land use practices have led to the growth of informal settlements. Although comprising a significant portion of the urban population, informal settlers lack access to basic services like water and sanitation, primarily because they lack land tenure. ADB's work on nature-based solutions for frontline urban services (e.g., sanitation, drainage, and flood prevention) in Makassar, Indonesia and in Suva, Fiji. These interventions demonstrate the effectiveness of a water-sensitive approach using decentralized green infrastructure to biologically treat contaminated and polluted water. Outcomes from these projects will help inform similar ADB projects in Bangladesh, Pakistan, and Viet Nam. They will also provide lessons on how to address land tenure issues in compact and densely populated informal settlements.

Technical assistance: **$1.05 million**

Operational Priority 2: Accelerating Progress in Gender Equality

Scaled-up support for gender equality; women's economic empowerment; gender equality in human development, decision-making, and leadership; reducing time poverty for women; strengthening women's resilience to shocks

Strategic Operational Priorities

1. **Women's economic empowerment increased**

2. **Gender equality in human development enhanced**

3. **Gender equality in decision-making and leadership enhanced**

4. **Women's time poverty and drudgery reduced**

5. **Women's resilience to external shocks strengthened**

Operational Approaches

- Scale-up gender mainstreaming in operations across sectors and themes

- Integrate Sustainable Development Goal (SDG) 5's "transformative" gender agenda, e.g., economic assets and resources for women, unpaid care and domestic work, digital technology and information and communication technology (ICT) and gender-based violence

- Expand gender mainstreaming in nonsovereign operations

- Tackle multiple gender inequalities through integrated solutions, e.g., livable cities program

- Develop capacity of developing member countries and clients in tracking and achieving gender-related SDGs

India: Modernizing Mumbai's Metro Rail System for the Safety and Security of Women, Children, and Disabled Persons

Safety remains a huge challenge in Mumbai's train system, with a large number of fatalities due to overcrowding, people falling from trains, and people crossing tracks. ADB is addressing these concerns through the Mumbai Metro Rail Systems Project, which is designed to reduce congestion on the existing suburban rail system and significantly improve passenger mobility and security. Utmost priority is given to ensuring that women, children, and disabled persons are always safe, from creating women-only coaches and mobile applications for women's security to installing instruction boards with helpline numbers and color-coded directional signs, priority e-ticket counters, reporting desks to address incidents of harassment, separate ticketing counters and vending machines, and a station staffed only by women. ADB also boosts women-led enterprises by implementing a quota system that ensures businesses owned or operated by women get a portion of commercial spaces in metro stations.

Loan: $926 million

Cofinancing, New Development Bank: $260 million

Pakistan: Opening Climate-Resilient Tourism Corridors and Boosting Women's Livelihoods

Pakistan is prone to disasters. Earthquakes, landslides, droughts, and floods are common, and climate change is making the situation worse. In 2014, floods devastated thousands of villages and killed hundreds of people. More than 2.5 million people were displaced by the disaster, and roads, basic services and livelihoods were washed away. Beyond providing critical emergency assistance, ADB helped rebuild 1,740 kilometers of provincial highways and district roads in accordance with climate-resilient standards, and rehabilitated 90% of the flood protection infrastructure . The intervention applied innovative smart bioengineering solutions to protect roads against landslides and empowered women who raised plant nurseries, thus promoting green enterprises and ecotourism.

Loan: $218.04 million

Technical assistance: $2 million

Armenia: Developing Entrepreneurship and Access to Finance for Women

Women in Armenia are not reaching their economic potential. Although educated, their ownership of enterprises and share of management positions are notoriously below regional averages, and their formal labor-force participation declined significantly during 2001 to 2012. ADB's intervention catalyzed women's entrepreneurship development. From 2013 to 2017, the number of firms whose ownership includes women grew from 32% to 34% and the number of firms with female top managers increased from 14% to 24%. Beyond enabling policy reforms and granting access to finance, ADB successfully implemented an effective outreach, training, and mentorship program that reached 204 women, enabled 79 to successfully register start-ups in 2013–2016, and obtained funding for 43 female entrepreneurs. Access to training and business development services, as well as raising awareness among women entrepreneurs, helped achieve gender equality results: by the end of 2017, 4,200 women benefited from business development services, and 2,040 loans were issued to women entrepreneurs. To further support women-led enterprises, ADB created gender-responsive loan guarantee schemes tailored to improve access to finance; 58 business start-ups led by women received loan guarantees for a total of $429,676.

Loan: $40 million

Technical assistance: $600,000

Operational Priority 3: Tackling Climate Change, Building Climate and Disaster Resilience, and Enhancing Environmental Sustainability

Low greenhouse gas emissions development, approach to building climate and disaster resilience, environmental sustainability, water–food–energy security nexus

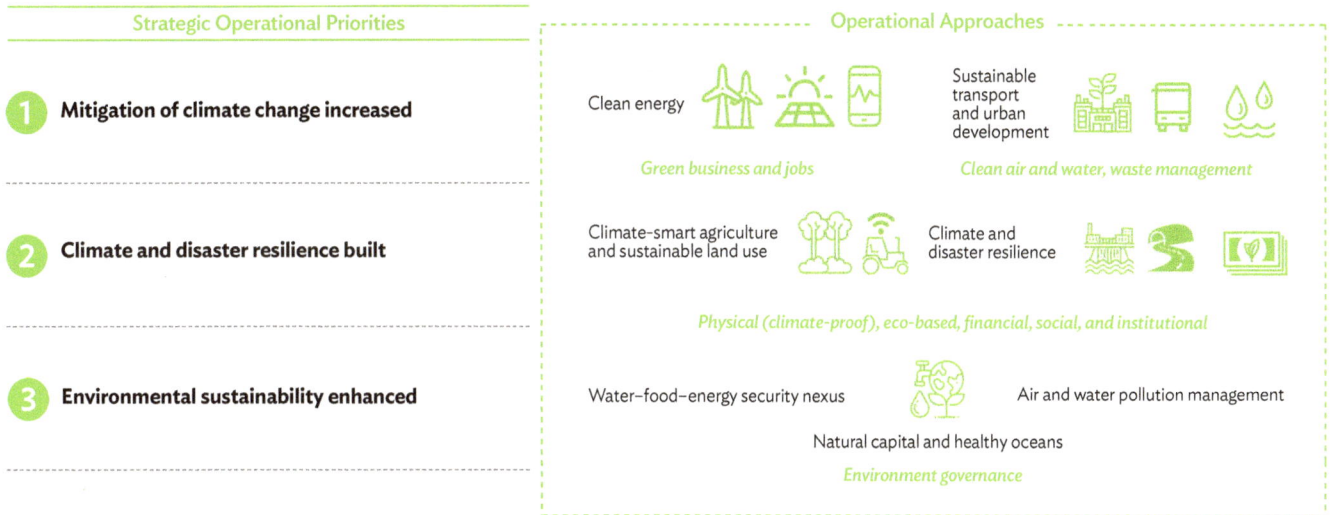

Strategic Operational Priorities

1 **Mitigation of climate change increased**

2 **Climate and disaster resilience built**

3 **Environmental sustainability enhanced**

Operational Approaches

Clean energy

Sustainable transport and urban development

Green business and jobs

Clean air and water, waste management

Climate-smart agriculture and sustainable land use

Climate and disaster resilience

Physical (climate-proof), eco-based, financial, social, and institutional

Water–food–energy security nexus

Air and water pollution management

Natural capital and healthy oceans

Environment governance

Myanmar: Improving Resilience and Livelihoods in Nearly 3,000 Rural Villages

Myanmar ranks among the highest countries in the 2020 Global Climate Risk Index. Disasters, triggered by natural hazards—floods, tropical cyclones, landslides, and droughts—threaten its population and economy. Aided by climate and disaster risk-modeling information, ADB is helping improve standards of living and increase resilience in 2,942 villages in the Ayeyarwady, Chin, Sagaing, and Tanintharyi regions. Cyclone shelters, water harvesting infrastructure, embankment and water management will be built; at least 15,000 climate-smart agriculture, livestock, and fisheries livelihood subprojects provided; and capacity around livelihood management, climate and disaster risk planning developed to benefit nearly 2 million people. A disaster contingency feature allows for immediate disbursement of reconstruction and livelihood recovery funds when a disaster affects an entire township.

Loan: **$195 million**

Tonga: Increasing Risk Resilience through Urban Infrastructure and Planning

With most of its atoll islands only 2–5 meters above sea level, the Kingdom of Tonga is the second most at-risk nation in the Pacific. Rising sea level, storm surge, cyclones, tsunamis, and climate change make its people, economy, and day-to-day operability extremely vulnerable. Employing an integrated approach, ADB is helping strengthen environmental and public health countrywide, especially in Nuku'alofa, the low-lying capital city, which houses critical infrastructure and services and more than 10,000 buildings. By helping manage the nexus of its solid waste, flood, and wastewater systems and developing a climate- and disaster-resilient urban development strategy and investment plan, ADB is helping ensure that Tonga can better respond to severe climate and disaster risks.

Grant: **$18.27 million**

Maldives: Creating a Healthy Living Environment through Sustainable Solid Waste Management

Behind its stunning beaches and vibrant marine life, the island nation of Maldives is waging a war against environmental waste. Due to inadequate collection and haphazard disposal of solid waste, the Greater Malé capital region and its outer islands suffer from chronic environmental pollution and deteriorating livability. Plumes of smoke from open burning of waste, visible from Malé, the international airport, and surrounding resorts compromise air quality, while toxic leachate contaminates soil and groundwater. Supported by ADB, a sustainable solid waste management system will improve waste collection, transfer, and disposal. The system will be made climate- and disaster-resilient through strengthened seawalls, raised floor elevations, enhanced drainage, and emergency planning. ADB is enhancing community-based island waste management systems on 32 inhabited outer islands covered by the project. The project is expected to benefit 216,000 people, or half of Maldives' population.

Grant: **$35.07 million** (Asian Development Fund: $33.07 million and Japan Fund for Poverty Reduction: $2.00 million)

Technical assistance: **$500,000**

India: Protecting and Sustainably Managing Karnataka's Coastline

The coastline of Karnataka supports vital fisheries, agriculture, tourism, ports, and major transport and communication sectors. Human and economic well-being and ecological integrity in the Indian state are under increasing threat from coastal erosion and climate change impacts. Because sustainable shoreline management is vital to the future of Karnataka's coastal regions, ADB and the Government of India are working to address immediate coastal protection needs and strengthen Karnataka's Infrastructure Development, Ports, and Inland Water Transport Departments. Eight subprojects will address medium to severe coastal erosion, protecting about 30 kilometers of coastline. Innovative coastal management techniques (e.g., artificial reefs, beach nourishment, and dune management) will benefit local communities and help address climate change concerns.

Loan: **$65.5 million**

Operational Priority 4: Making Cities More Livable

Integrated solutions, funding for cities, inclusive and participatory urban planning, climate resilience and disaster management

Strategic Operational Priorities

1 Improve coverage, quality, efficiency, and reliability of services in urban areas

2 Strengthen urban planning and financial sustainability of cities

3 Improve urban environment, climate resilience, and disaster management of cities

Operational Approaches

- Build capacities and strengthen institutions
- Foster integrated city development
- Combine policy reforms, capacity development, institutional strengthening, and knowledge management
- Develop pilots and leapfrog to the latest technologies
- Prepare and implement smart city plans
- Enhance city competitiveness and productivity
- Support localization and implementation of Sustainable Development Goals

- Support infrastructure and services in urban areas
- Scale-up the use of proven digital technologies (e.g. ADB's Spatial Data Analysis Explorer or SPADE)
- Ensure water security and adequate waste management
- Provide energy security
- Promote public mass transport
- Support pro-poor and inclusive cities with social services, and safe and healthy urban environments

- Prepare integrated urban plans
- Support inclusive and participatory planning
- Use differentiated approaches to different categories of cities

- Support cities to maximize their internal financial resources
- Promote land-based financing
- Develop innovative external sources of financing
- Support utilities and service providers to develop public–private partnerships
- Support urban governance improvement of utilities

- Support environment improvement projects
- Promote energy-efficient and environment-friendly technologies and processes
- Support risk-sensitive land use management
- Promote circular economy practices
- Adopt nature-based solutions

- Support resilient cities
- Strengthen disaster preparedness and emergency response plans
- Support cities to localize nationally determined contributions
- Adopt a systems approach to urban infrastructure resilience

Mongolia: Transforming Polluted *Ger* Areas into Affordable, Low-Carbon, and Resilient EcoDistricts

In the fringes of Ulaanbaatar, an approximately 100-square kilometer sprawl of traditional *ger* tents and individual houses cloaks the surrounding hills. Home to about 850,000 people(60% of Ulaanbaatar's population, one-third of Mongolia's population, and including many traditional herders fleeing poor rural living condition, severe winters, and summer droughts), *ger* areas suffer from poor sanitation due to open pit latrines, poor solid waste collection, traffic congestion, and limited access to potable water. Heavy reliance on coal stoves for heating and energy generates large carbon dioxide emissions, worsening already severe air pollution in winter. An 8-year ADB project is introducing the city's first public–private–people partnership, an integrated design solution to transform the substandard, climate-vulnerable, and heavily polluting *ger* areas into affordable, low-carbon, climate-resilient, and livable ecodistricts. The project will leverage private-sector investment to deliver 10,000 affordable green housing units, and redevelop 100 hectares of *ger* areas into mixed-use, and mixed-income vibrant and green ecodistricts. The project has the potential to set a new precedent on the linkage between urbanization, affordable housing, climate change, and climate risk.

ADB loans and grant: $83 million

Cofinancing The Green Climate Fund (GCF)Loan: $95 million

Grant: $50 million   Private sector and beneficiary: $307.1 million

People's Republic of China: Piloting "Sponge Cities" to Reduce Flood Risk

In many cities in Asia, monsoon and typhoon seasons deliver huge rainfall to impervious concrete surfaces that block the natural flow of water, quickly converting rainfall to surface runoff that overwhelms drainage systems and causes flooding. Inadequate sewer and wastewater treatment systems overflow, affecting water quality and public health. In the People's Republic of China (PRC), a new "sponge cities" approach uses green infrastructure to absorb, harvest, store, filter, purify, and slowly release rainwater, like a sponge. Early test areas show an 85 % reduction in annual runoff, mitigating floods while purifying, conserving, and recharging groundwater for later use. ADB is piloting the "sponge cities" concept in the flood-prone city of Pingxiang, Jiangxi province, integrating river rehabilitation with flood risk management by protecting floodplains, restoring wetlands, and creating wide green spaces along rivers to make Pingxiang more water secure, livable, and green.

Loan: $150 million

Viet Nam: Mainstreaming Green and Resilient Urban Development in Secondary Cities

Urbanization in Viet Nam is rapidly rising, and more than 30 million people now live in cities. However, the benefits of urbanization are uneven. In secondary cities (e.g., Hue in central Viet Nam and Vinh Yen and Ha Giang up north), less than 60% of households are connected to water supply systems and only 10% of wastewater is centrally treated. The dire lack of basic infrastructure and services makes these cities vulnerable to climate change and health impacts. ADB is introducing green infrastructure solutions, including an ecological and climate-resilient design for embankments and urban drainage channels that will minimize concrete structures, balance engineering measures with river ecosystem conservation, and enhance public amenities. Project data on the three cities are stored in ADB's Spatial Data Analysis Explorer (SPADE) platform to better inform future project design and investments, factoring in climate hazards and resilience across urban and multiple other sectors. About 116,000 households currently benefit from better living conditions in Hue, Vinh Yen, and Ha Giang. ADB is working to replicate the same approach in other secondary cities across Viet Nam.

Loan: $170 million

Operational Priority 5: Promoting Rural Development and Food

Market connectivity and agricultural value chain linkages, agricultural productivity and food security, food safety

Strategic Operational Priorities

1 **Rural development**

2 **Agricultural value chains**

3 **Food security**

Operational Approaches

- Rural–urban connectivity
- Rural health and education
- Rural economic hubs
- Modern agricultural value chains
- Off-grid energy solutions
- Food safety and traceability
- Affordable rural finance
- Climate-smart agriculture
- Water service delivery and efficiency
- Water–food–health nexus
- Youth and women empowerment
- Knowledge-intensive agriculture

Lao People's Democratic Republic: Providing Sustainable Infrastructure and Watershed Management

Rural poverty runs high in the northern provinces of the Lao People's Democratic Republic, where poverty rates are three times higher than in cities. As men seek work in urban areas, more women are left to live on low returns from rice farming, highly vulnerable to volatile commodity prices, losing their land through concessions, and ill health from poor diets and sanitation.

By strengthening agriculture, irrigation, infrastructure, and nutrition, ADB is helping create jobs and improve livelihoods and health in four northern provinces: Houaphan, Louangphabang, Xaignabouli, and Xiangkhouang. Agricultural grants to producers and entrepreneurs and access to new climate-resilient technologies, will help develop diverse, market-oriented agricultural products, particularly high-value crops. Key components of the project include protecting watersheds to increase flood and drought resilience and establishing 100 nutrition schools to help meet the nutritional needs of 9,400 adolescent girls and women of reproductive age.

Loan: **$40 million**

Afghanistan: Stable and Well-Managed Water Resources for Agriculture

Water supply in Afghanistan is scarce and highly seasonal. The lack of well-managed integrated water resources, especially of reliable irrigation water, greatly affects the country's agriculture sector, a major source of livelihood that employed 62.2% of its labor force in 2017, and it hinders the sector's huge potential and further contribution to the economy. In 2019, ADB approved the Arghandab Integrated Water Resources Development Project to help improve management and use of water resources in the Arghandab River.

The project aims to improve Afghanistan's agricultural productivity, energy generation, and growth outlook. Under the project, the storage capacity of the Dahla Dam, the country's second-largest dam, will be increased and its operations improved, canals and structures upgraded, irrigation infrastructure of the Arghandab Irrigation System improved, community irrigation infrastructure rehabilitated, and monitoring and control systems introduced to allow water-on-demand services in the province. Female farmers will also be empowered through increased training opportunities, scholarships, technology transfer, and advisory services.

Grant: **$348.78 million**

People's Republic of China: Securing Sustainable Economic Growth in the Yangtze River Green Ecological Corridor

As the third-longest river in the world, the Yangtze flows through the eastern, central, and western parts of the PRC, covering more than 2 million square kilometers. Teeming with natural resources, the Yangtze is one of the PRC's three key growth engines; it is also the most problematic. Agricultural production systems are far from sustainable: 92% of nitrogen discharged into the river comprise agricultural nonpoint source pollution, impeding not only productivity, human health, and natural resources, but also sustainable economic development. ADB is using innovative solutions to help modernize agricultural production, reduce pollution, improve soil and water conservation, and upgrade irrigation and drainage infrastructure, making e-farming operations more sustainable. Investing in the green corridor will benefit more than 168,000 people, particularly the rural poor. Establishing integrated water resources management in six watersheds of the Yangtze River Basin will help improve environmental protection, rehabilitation, and sustainable management of the Yangtze River.

Loan: **$300 million**

Beneficiaries: **$33.1 million**

Operational Priority 6: Strengthening Governance and Institutional Capacity

Public management reforms and financial sustainability, service delivery, capacity and standards

Strategic Operational Priorities

1 Public management and financial stability enhanced

2 Governance and institutional capacity for service delivery improved

3 Country systems and standards effectively utilized

Operational Approaches

- Domestic resources mobilization
- Public financial management, expenditure and fiscal policies, adequate fiscal space for service delivery
- Support for private sector development
- Macro-fiscal stability
- Strengthened subnational governments capacity
- Sate-Owned Enterprise (SOE) reforms
- Improved legal and judicial institutional capacity
- Strengthened financial management and procurement systems
- Anticorruption and integrity measures
- Strong statistical institutions
- Environmental and social safeguards
- Differentiated approaches in fragile and conflict-affected situations

Law and Policy Reform: Strengthening Inclusive Development

Good governance anchored on the rule of law relies on effective judicial, regulatory, and administrative institutions that establish, implement, and enforce laws fairly, consistently, and ethically.

For nearly 25 years, ADB's Law and Policy Reform (LPR) Program has strengthened the quality of laws and regulations and the effectiveness of legal systems in its DMCs and also built the capacity of their institutions. ADB support has led to efficiency, transparency, and integrity in the areas of Anti-Money Laundering/Combating the Financing of Terrorism (AML/CFT), private sector development, gender equality, and environmental and climate governance.

For example, ADB's LPR work to enhance the capacity of Asian judiciaries to adjudicate environmental and climate change disputes resulted in the establishment of green courts, judicial certification programs on environment, and the introduction of new environmental court procedures. Additionally, ADB is helping DMCs establish the necessary legal and regulatory frameworks, create enabling environments to meet mitigation commitments and adaptation needs under the Paris Agreement, and attract more international climate finance and investments.

Promoting Anticorruption and Integrity

Assessing and managing integrity risks is essential to ensuring that ADB resources are used for their intended purposes. Between 2018 and 2019, investigations led ADB to debar 149 firms (80 in 2018 and 69 in 2019) and 87 individuals (25 in 2018 and 62 in 2019) for violating its Anticorruption Policy. Pursuant to the Agreement for Mutual Enforcement of Debarment Decisions. (GRI Disclosure 205 and 205-3), ADB cross-debarred 425 firms in 2018 and 68 individuals in 2019, after receiving notifications from other participating international financial institutions.

In 2018 and 2019, ADB provided capacity development support to Bhutan, Mongolia, Papua New Guinea, the Philippines, and Viet Nam to help these DMCs comply with AML/CFT standards.

ADB also shared best practices for the G20's "Good Practices Guide on Promoting Integrity and Transparency in Infrastructure Development" and co-hosted the 10th Regional Conference on Preventing and Combating Corruption in Infrastructure Projects under the Anticorruption Initiative for Asia and the Pacific—the largest anticorruption network in the region.

Operational Priority 7: Fostering Regional Cooperation and Integration

Connectivity and competitiveness, regional public goods, cooperation in finance sector, subregional initiatives

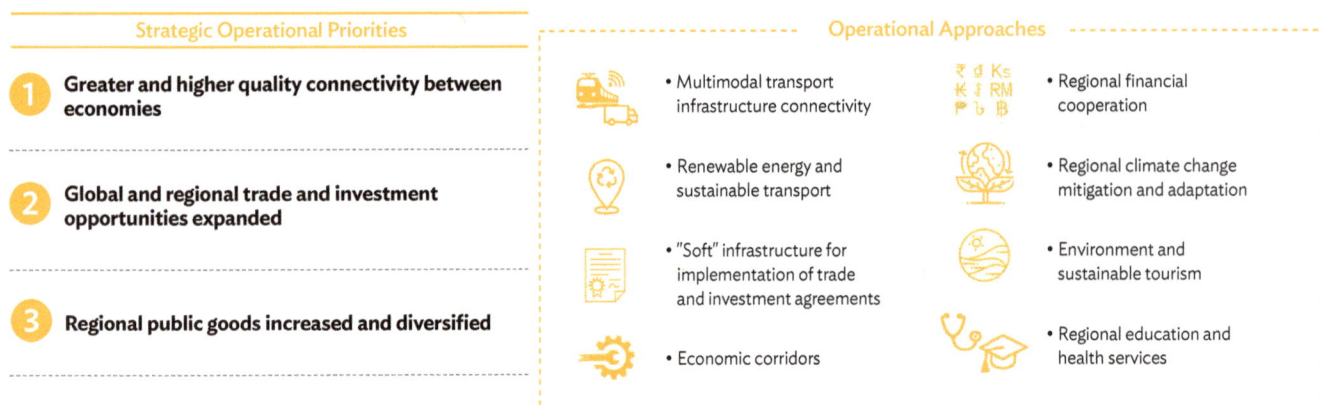

Strategic Operational Priorities

1 Greater and higher quality connectivity between economies

2 Global and regional trade and investment opportunities expanded

3 Regional public goods increased and diversified

Operational Approaches

- Multimodal transport infrastructure connectivity
- Renewable energy and sustainable transport
- "Soft" infrastructure for implementation of trade and investment agreements
- Economic corridors
- Regional financial cooperation
- Regional climate change mitigation and adaptation
- Environment and sustainable tourism
- Regional education and health services

Uniting the Greater Mekong Subregion around Green Growth, Environmental Cooperation, and Public Health

Greater Mekong Subregion: The Core Environment Program Strategic Framework and Action Plan, 2018–2022

In 2018, environment ministers from the six countries in the Greater Mekong Subregion (GMS)—Cambodia, the PRC (specifically Yunnan Province and Guangxi Zhuang Autonomous Region), the Lao PDR, Myanmar, Thailand, and Viet Nam—endorsed a 5-year strategic framework and action plan. In 2019, ADB approved a technical assistance (TA) for the GMS Climate Change and Environmental Sustainability Program (TA 9915) to support implementation of the action plan until 2025. The TA will create enabling conditions to generate knowledge and leverage investments in (i) building climate and disaster resilience; (ii) facilitating low-carbon transitions; (iii) promoting climate-smart landscapes; (iv) enhancing environmental quality through pollution control and sustainable waste management; (v) deploying digital technologies for climate actions and environmental sustainability; and (vi) financing low-carbon and climate-resilient infrastructure and technologies, including demonstrating climate and disaster risk-financing instruments.

Since its launch in 2006, the ADB-administered program has helped lift over 30,000 people from rural poverty. It raised over $100 million in additional financing, including $98 million for biodiversity and conservation; created 2.6 million hectares of biodiversity corridors in 7 transboundary landscapes; and trained more than 19,000 stakeholders.

Greater Mekong Subregion Health Cooperation Strategy, 2019–2023

In 2019, the Ministry of Health of each GMS country endorsed a unified strategy for health cooperation for the next 5 years. This strategy includes addressing regional public goods for health security, increasing health service access for migrant and mobile populations, and enhancing human resource capacity to respond to priority health issues.

Central Asia Cities: Promoting Sustainable, Low-Carbon Development

With urbanization rising within countries under the Central Asia Regional Economic Cooperation (CAREC) program, key cities are feeling the benefits of improved livelihood opportunities and economic growth. However, much of the region's urban development has been left unchecked, and these cities are now dealing with worsening pollution, depletion of energy and natural resources, and rising greenhouse gas emissions and other air pollutants. For example, in Kazakhstan's capital city Nur-Sultan, where during cold winter days (as low as -35°C), citizens idle their car engines unnecessarily, wasting fuel, costing money, causing excess engine wear and tear, and increasing harmful air pollutants, ADB helped introduce a new engine block heater technology, which could achieve a net fuel reduction of over 220 million liters and also reduce carbon emissions by 430,000 tons per year. ADB is also helping prepare its low-carbon development strategy until 2050, introducing a new approach to decarbonization of different sectors.

Similar interventions promoting sustainable, low-carbon city development will support other CAREC countries, like Mongolia and the PRC, in meeting their nationally determined contribution (NDC) targets under the Paris Agreement.

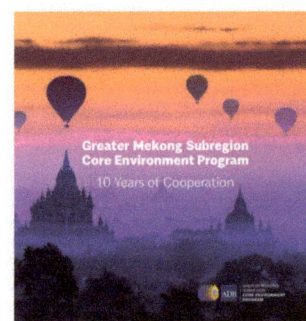

VII. ENVIRONMENTAL AND SOCIAL SAFEGUARDS

ADB's environmental and social safeguards are a cornerstone of its support for inclusive economic growth and environmental sustainability in Asia and the Pacific. Since 1979, ADB has required environmental assessments. ADB then introduced policies relating to involuntary resettlement, indigenous peoples, and the environment. ADB's current Safeguards Policy Statement (SPS) (2009) builds upon the three previous safeguard policies and brings them into a consolidated policy framework that enhances effectiveness and relevance. The SPS aims to promote sustainable project outcomes by protecting the environment and people from potential adverse impacts by (i) avoiding adverse impacts of projects on the environment and affected people, where possible; and (ii) minimizing, mitigating, and/or compensating for adverse impacts when avoidance is not possible. Policy implementation involves a structured process of impact assessment, planning, and mitigation to address the adverse impacts of projects throughout their life cycles. Safeguard documents are disclosed to the general public in a form, manner, and language accessible to them, and the information is updated as necessary during the project cycle.

Under the SPS, ADB aims to help borrowers and/or clients strengthen their safeguard systems and develop the capacity to manage environmental and social risks. All ADB investment projects are screened and categorized on a sliding scale of A to C, based on the significance of potential impacts or risks, or categorized as financial intermediary at the project identification stage.

In 2020, ADB's Independent Evaluation Department completed a review of the effectiveness of the 2009 SPS. Findings and recommendations from the evaluation are helping guide the ongoing update of ADB's safeguard policy.

ADB will not finance projects that

- do not comply with its Safeguard Policy Statement;
- do not comply with the host country's social and environmental laws and regulations, including laws implementing host country obligations under international law; and
- include activities on the prohibited investments list. (as defined in Annex V of the Safeguard Policy Statement)

Three Key Safeguards

Project category (2018–2019)   A ■   B ■   C ■   FI ■

1. Environmental

Environmental safeguards are triggered if a project is likely to have environmental impacts and risks, including biodiversity protection and sustainable natural resource management, pollution prevention and abatement, health and safety, and physical cultural resources.

28	10%
141	53%
62	23%
38	14%

2. Involuntary resettlement

Involuntary resttelement safeguards focus on situations that involve either involuntary acquisition of land or involuntary restrictions on land use, resulting in physical or economic displacement.

25	9%
71	27%
135	50%
38	14%

3. Indigenous peoples

Safeguards for indigenous peoples are triggered if a project directly or indirectly affects their dignity, human rights, livelihood systems, or culture; or affects the territories of natural or cultural resources they own, use, occupy, or claim as an ancestral domain or asset.

1	0%
40	15%
190	71%
38	14%

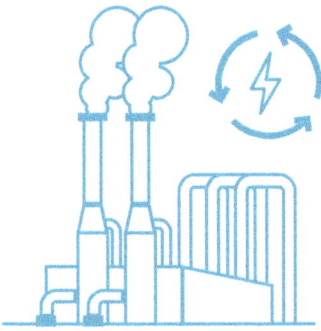

Bangladesh: Modifying Power Plant Design to Protect Health and Biodiversity

Providing reliable and affordable energy remains a challenge for Bangladesh, which experiences frequent load-shedding and seasonal power cuts that affect industrial growth. ADB is helping address rising energy demand with construction of a state-of-the-art 800-megawatt gas-fired plant that uses highly efficient, cleaner technology. To respond to monitoring results of the plant's environmental and impact assessments on air and water quality, the community, and surrounding biodiversity, changes needed to be made to the plant's design.

A low-nitrogen oxide burner was added to reduce expected emissions by 60%. Adopting zero-discharge technology also minimized the anticipated impacts of the plant's water consumption and discharge on endangered Ganges River dolphins in the adjacent river. The plant's location at the abandoned Khulna Newsprint Mills minimizes land acquisition and resettlement impacts, while a grievance redress mechanism, accessible to the surrounding community, was established to address affected people's concerns promptly, using an understandable and transparent process.

Loan: $500 million   Grant: $1.5 million

Southern Bhutan: Preventing Adverse Impacts to Wildlife

Asia's immense biodiversity is increasingly under threat from road and railway projects expanding across the region. When poorly planned, such projects lead to the loss and fragmentation of pristine natural habitats and wildlife sanctuaries, while creating barriers to the movement of wildlife.

Along the Himalayan foothills in Southern Bhutan, endangered elephants migrate freely through dense forests to the Indian border, using streams and riverbeds as their regular feeding routes, and travel long distances and back in search of food, minerals, and water. To avoid and mitigate negative impacts on elephant migration and their access to various habitats, an ADB road network project along the Southern border designed and constructed eight wildlife underpasses. These underpasses allowed the elephants and other wildlife to move safely under the road, reducing collision risks. Infrared camera traps showed high usage by elephants and other species, including gaur (Indian bison) and deer. In addition, the alignment of one road was shifted by 500 meters to avoid anticipated impacts on Oyster Lake, a known watering hole for wildlife and a sacred community worship site.

Lessons from the Bhutan project will inform and influence decision-making in similar or better wildlife crossings regarding follow-up road and railways projects that pass through pristine natural habitats and host a number of charismatic and globally threatened species including the Asian elephant, Bengal tiger, and rufous-necked hornbill.

VIII. PRIVATE SECTOR OPERATIONS

ADB continues to devise innovative approaches to mobilize and maximize the potential of private enterprises to address the challenges facing Asia and the Pacific. We are set to scale-up private sector operations to reach one-third of total operations in terms of number of projects by 2024.

ADB's private sector operations set a record in 2018, with investments increasing to $3.1 billion vs. $2.3 billion in 2017 and $1.8 billion in 2016. The energy sector and financial institutions accounted for 67% of new projects committed in 2018, comprising several landmark transactions in geothermal energy; climate and green bonds; green bus leasing; and micro, small, and medium-sized enterprise financing. Areas that previously had lesser focus (e.g., agribusiness and non-energy infrastructure) increased their share to 20%. In 2019, ADB committed private sector investments for 38 projects across 16 DMCs plus 7 regional projects for a total of $3.0 billion. ADB also generated a record $6.98 billion in commercial cofinancing in 2019, almost half of which was on long-term cofinancing.

In 2020, ADB approved its Operational Plan for Private Sector Operations 2019–2024, which outlines how private sector operations will contribute to Strategy 2030's operational priorities and focus on increasing private sector operations in health, agribusiness, and education. It envisions that ADB will continue supporting core infrastructure and finance investments while also venturing into areas of infrastructure beyond energy, such as environmental infrastructure, transport, and information and communication technology.

Guided by the five-year plan, ADB will further sharpen its investment focus on an increasing share of complex, highly innovative, smaller, and riskier projects in challenging markets and sectors, including fragile and conflicted-affected situations, and enhance already considerable efforts to address climate change and support women.

Figure 2: Results Achieved by ADB's Active Private Sector Portfolio

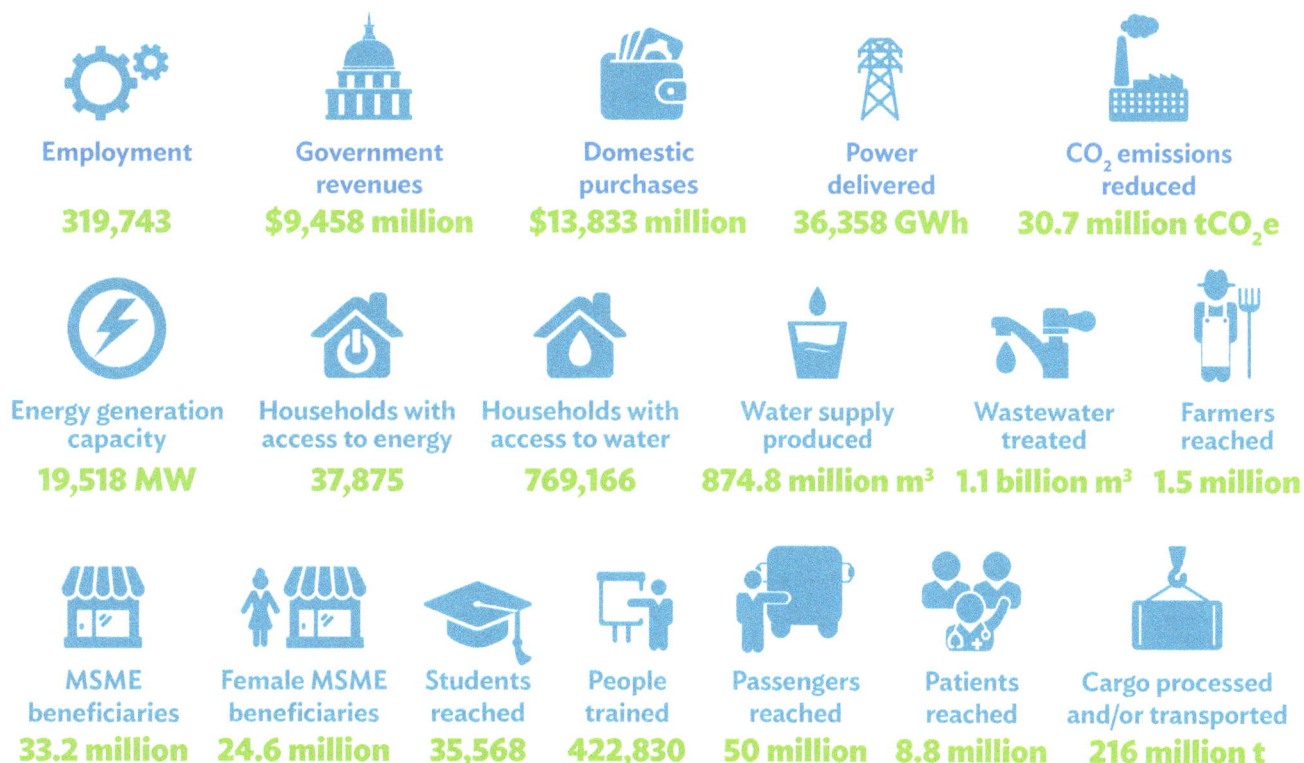

Employment	**Government revenues**	**Domestic purchases**	**Power delivered**	**CO_2 emissions reduced**
319,743	$9,458 million	$13,833 million	36,358 GWh	30.7 million tCO_2e
Energy generation capacity	**Households with access to energy**	**Households with access to water**	**Water supply produced**	**Wastewater treated** / **Farmers reached**
19,518 MW	37,875	769,166	874.8 million m^3	1.1 billion m^3 / 1.5 million
MSME beneficiaries	**Female MSME beneficiaries**	**Students reached**	**People trained**	**Passengers reached** / **Patients reached** / **Cargo processed and/or transported**
33.2 million	24.6 million	35,568	422,830	50 million / 8.8 million / 216 million t

CO_2 = carbon dioxide; tCO_2e = tons of carbon dioxide equivalent; GWh = gigawatt-hour; m^3 = cubic meter; MSME = micro, small, and medium-sized enterprise; MW – megawatt; PSOD = Private Sector Operations Department; t = ton.
Source: Asian Development Bank (Private Sector Operations Department).

IX. KNOWLEDGE SERVICES

Developing member countries (DMCs) turn to ADB for project design and implementation; the transfer of technology and best practices; and the sharing of knowledge, skills, and expertise accumulated over more than 50 years of working in Asia and the Pacific. ADB's expertise in safeguard policies for environmental and social impacts, procurement, economic research, treasury operations, legal affairs, risk management, fragile and conflict-affected situations, and independent evaluation are all essential sources of its knowledge services to DMCs. Our sector and thematic groups, regional departments, and Knowledge Advisory Services Center drive our knowledge work.

ADB regularly uses regional and national conferences and other events to share its knowledge products and exchange views with government officials and other key audiences. ADB also participates in regional and global forums (e.g., ASEAN+3, the World Cities Summit, and the Conference of the Parties [COP]) during which DMCs request support from ADB.

In 2018 and 2019, ADB strengthened its programmatic knowledge, published knowledge products, and hosted important knowledge-exchange forums on climate and disaster risk resilience, clean energy, sustainable transport, water, climate actions, and digital transformation, among others.

Improving Air Quality in Urban Asia

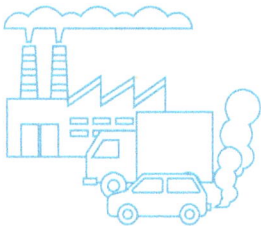

Air pollution is now Asia's most pressing environmental concern and a leading preventable cause of death. Unhealthy levels of indoor and outdoor air pollution adversely affect the environment, human health, and quality of life in more than 90% of the region's cities, choking their economic prospects.

While countries and cities are unique, they share many common challenges in air quality management, including weak institutions; inappropriate policies; lack of awareness on the true impacts and costs of air pollution; inefficient, polluting technologies and lack of access to cleaner technologies; and absence of supporting regulations, fiscal incentives, and standards, among others.

Lessons and successful strategies from other Asian cities can help achieve better air quality. ADB has been working with Ricardo and Clean Air Asia to enhance the knowledge and capacity of cities in Bangladesh, Mongolia, Pakistan, the Philippines, and Viet Nam around knowledge, policy actions, and technological solutions for better air quality management. This support will include conducting city-level air quality studies; identifying measures and innovative technologies, policy recommendations, and capacity support; and supporting preparation of city-level clean air action plans with investment estimates to implement them effectively.

Protecting and Investing in Natural Capital

Natural capital refers to the stock of natural ecosystems and services, including (i) renewable natural ecosystems and resources, (ii) nonrenewable resources, and (iii) ecosystem services. Combined with unprecedented urbanization, agriculture, and infrastructure expansion, overexploitation of Asia's forests, rangeland, oceans, coasts, fresh water, and wildlife has led to massive declines in biodiversity, thus increasing water and food insecurity and climate vulnerability.

Through technical assistance (TA), ADB supports DMCs with knowledge and technical expertise to build the business case for investments to restore, protect, and sustainably manage natural capital. This includes the development of guiding principles, planning tools, and building the capacity of engineers around ecologically sensitive transport infrastructure in partnership with the Wildlife Institute of India.

Key initiatives include support for integrating nature-based solutions into flood risk master planning in the Philippines and Indonesia, mainstreaming green urban design guidelines in New Clark City, Philippines, revitalizing Pakistan's polluted River Ravi, and combating illegal wildlife trade in the Philippines in partnership with the Global Environment Facility.

Road ecology website and app captures roadkill and live observations and local knowledge in wildlife corridors in Nepal.

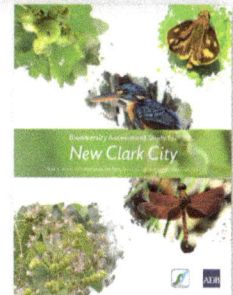

NDC Advance: Accelerating Climate Actions in Asia and the Pacific

NDC Advance is a dedicated technical assistance platform established in 2018 to help ADB's developing member countries (DMCs) mobilize finance, build capacity, and provide knowledge and other support needed to implement their nationally determined contributions (NDCs).

NDC Advance will

- help DMCs refine and enhance their ambition, translate NDCs into climate investment plans, and identify priority climate projects that may be executed with ADB assistance;
- improve DMC access to external public and private actors who support the use of innovative finance mechanisms to secure needed financing; and
- develop methods and tools to measure, monitor, and report on commitments made under NDCs.

X. ENHANCING HUMAN RESOURCES

By the end of 2019, ADB employed 3,555 staff across its headquarters and 43 field offices comprising 25 resident missions, the Philippines Country Office, the Pacific Liaison and Coordination Office, the ADB office in Singapore, the Pacific Subregional Office, 11 Pacific Country Offices, and three Representative Offices in Donor Members. Among these, 2,636 staff (74%) were based in headquarters and 919 (26%) were based in field offices. *(GRI Disclosure 102-7 and 102-8)*

ADB's staff values, as set out in its staff Code of Conduct (Administrative Order 2.02, 2017), include respect for clients, professionalism, work ethics and integrity, respect for diversity, commitment to achieving poverty reduction in Asia and the Pacific through development effectiveness, collaboration, and responsibility.

ADB requires staff to maintain a high degree of integrity, conduct themselves in a manner befitting their status as international civil servants, and act in ADB's institutional interest in their work.

Upon appointment, staff affirm in writing that they will conduct their responsibilities in a manner that will further the purpose of ADB, abide by the Staff Regulations, and accept no instruction in performing their duties from any government or authority external to ADB. Staff are required to annually certify that their actions comply with, among others, ADB's

- Staff Regulations,
- Staff Code of Conduct (2017),
- Anticorruption Policy (1998), and
- Integrity Principles and Guidelines (2015).

Career Development

ADB is committed to the growth and development of all staff. We empower our people to perform at their highest potential by supporting them in their roles and investing in their training and development across operations, leadership, management, innovation, and digital technologies. All staff have access to high-quality e-learning, in-house programs, and ADB-funded external learning opportunities. We encourage and support collaboration across the organization to ensure that the collective capacity of our staff is brought to bear upon the complex challenges faced by our organization and clients. ADB holds midyear and annual performance reviews. *(GRI Disclosure 404, 404-1, and 404-2)*

Diversity and Inclusion

Diversity, inclusion, and belonging are fundamental elements of ADB's culture and core to enabling us to deliver on our mission. We believe that having a workforce with diverse backgrounds, experiences, and points of view contributes to developing innovative and sustainable development solutions. We actively support gender equality, increasing the representation of female staff in our international workforce to 37%, and have expanded our focus on lesbian, gay, bisexual, and transgender (LGBT) + inclusion. We understand that respect and inclusion help us create a welcoming, engaging, and collaborative environment for all. An independent gender pay gap study, commissioned by ADB, showed no significant or unexplained gaps in pay between women and men in comparable roles at ADB. *(GRI Disclosure 401 and 405)*

Figure 3: Profile of Staff by Employment Category and Gender, 2018 to 2019 (number and %)

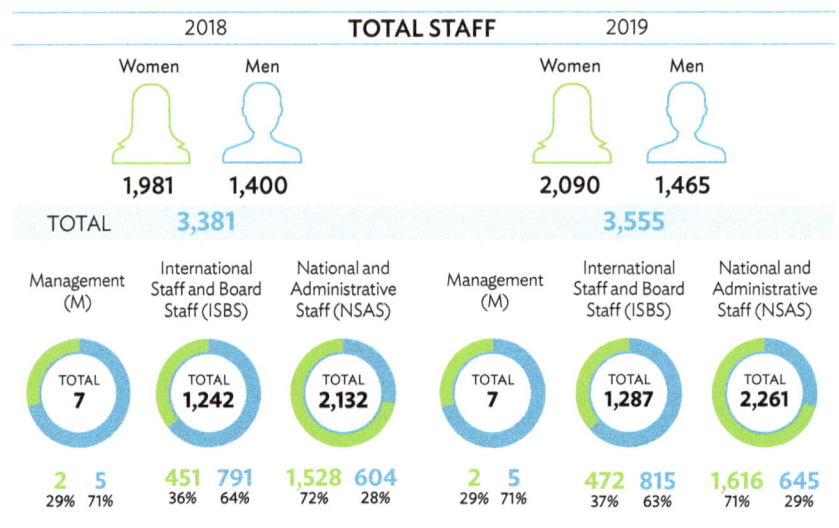

	2018		**TOTAL STAFF**	2019	
	Women	Men		Women	Men
	1,981	1,400		2,090	1,465
TOTAL	**3,381**			**3,555**	

Management (M)	International Staff and Board Staff (ISBS)	National and Administrative Staff (NSAS)	Management (M)	International Staff and Board Staff (ISBS)	National and Administrative Staff (NSAS)
TOTAL 7	TOTAL 1,242	TOTAL 2,132	TOTAL 7	TOTAL 1,287	TOTAL 2,261
2 / 5	451 / 791	1,528 / 604	2 / 5	472 / 815	1,616 / 645
29% / 71%	36% / 64%	72% / 28%	29% / 71%	37% / 63%	71% / 29%

Figure 4: Average Hours of Training, 2018 to 2019

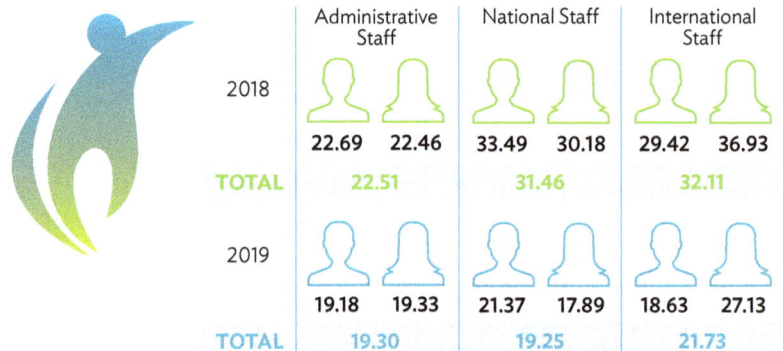

	Administrative Staff		National Staff		International Staff	
2018	22.69	22.46	33.49	30.18	29.42	36.93
TOTAL	22.51		31.46		32.11	
2019	19.18	19.33	21.37	17.89	18.63	27.13
TOTAL	19.30		19.25		21.73	

Workforce Integrity

ADB is a talent-driven business that understands the most important element influencing employee satisfaction and productivity boils down to one thing: a good and respectful work environment. From in-house staff to consultants and contractors, we continue to advocate for the rights, welfare, and benefits of our over 3,500-strong workforce through the ADB Code of Conduct, as well as programs and initiatives that ensure our workplace remains free from harassment, bullying, discrimination, and other forms of grievances. ADB's Office of Professional Conduct (OPC) was established in 2019 to support an enabling environment for a positive, professional work environment in ADB in line with ADB's Code of Conduct.
(GRI Disclosure 102–16, 401, 405, 406, and 406–1)

Safety and Security

Competitive, locally-relevant health, medical, and disability benefits; employee medical care services; and compliance to international Occupational Health and Safety Management System standards combine to deliver on ADB's promise of providing a safe and healthy working environment. ADB also ensures that employees deployed on mission travel have 24/7 access to the ADB Incident Coordinator. Health and recreational activities are widely encouraged to promote good health, well-being, and facilitate interaction among the staff.
(GRI Disclosure 403-1, 403-5, 403-6, 403-9, and 403-10)

Table 1: Number of Workplace Matters Reviewed

		2018	2019	Total
Matters reviewed		125	110	235
Cases reviewed		52	45	97

Pertaining to staff concerns on bullying, harassment and other misconduct.

Figure 5: First Aid, Emergency Family Preparedness and Fire and Safety Prevention Trainings, 2018–2019

2018
54 ISO Orientations
2,279 participants

3 First Aid Trainings	43 Total Participants
2 Family Preparedness Emergency Sessions	44 Total Participants
6 Fire Safety and Prevention Trainings	215 Total Participants

2019
34 ISO Orientations
2,081 participants

5 First Aid Trainings	108 Total Participants
5 Family Preparedness Emergency Sessions	85 Total Participants
6 Fire Safety and Prevention Trainings	119 Total Participants

ISO = International Organization for Standardization.

The Asian Development Bank (ADB) headquarters in Mandaluyong City, Metro Manila, Philippines. ADB staff entering through the Guadix Drive gate, riding bicycles to work.

XI. RESOURCE MANAGEMENT

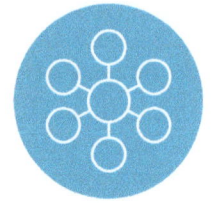

Elevating Sustainability Standards in Asia and the Pacific

ADB is always looking for ways to make our community a better place to work and live. We are the first multilateral development bank (MDB) to achieve certifications in International Organization for Standardization (ISO) 14001, ISO 50001, and Occupational Health and Safety Assessment Series (OHSAS) 18001, and earn and sustain Leadership in Energy and Environmental Design (LEED) gold certification for operating and maintaining green buildings in ADB headquarters. It is especially gratifying that these achievements come during a time of increasing staff numbers, resulting in rising business travel and additional pressure on resource consumption and waste generation. Our success has served as a model for others and a springboard for continued accomplishment.

ADB was the first MDB to voluntarily achieve ISO and OHSAS certifications in energy, environment, and health and safety management systems for its headquarters.

ADB's E2HSMS has been certified to international management system standards since 2003.

E2HSMS

1 Compliance with Legal Requirements
2 Pollution Prevention
3 Resource Conservation
4 Enhanced Health and Safety
5 Involvement through Information Dissemination
6 Continual Improvement

Occupational Health and Safety

Successfully transitioned to the new standard ISO 45001

Previously certified under OHSAS 18001 (Certification audit completed in 2018)

Environmental Management

Successfully transitioned to the new version ISO 14001:2015

Previously certified under ISO 14001:2004 (Certification audit completed in 2018)

ADB invests in sound environmental and natural resource management while promoting green growth, low-carbon development, and adaptation to climate change. We continually work hard to maintain our certifications and reduce the impact of our activities and operations.

ADB has solar panels with installed capacity of **689 kW** providing approximately **3.6%** of ADB headquarters' electricity needs.

Building skylights provide natural lighting, saving energy.

Practicing Water Efficiency

Rainwater-harvesting facility and use of treated water from sewage treatment plant provides water for cleaning the building and watering plants and toilet-flushing.

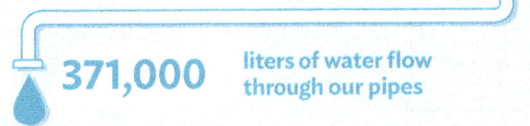

371,000 liters of water flow through our pipes

Heat reduction from tree shading of open car parks and easy access to public transportation from ADB Headquarters.

ADB solid waste segregation recovers recyclable materials, which are then sold to recyclers.

Green procurement strives to attain local and sustainable goods and services, where feasible.

Water Conservation

daily savings vs. current fixtures at **~32,000 gallons per day** **21%**

Water fixtures (Completed in 2018)

579 units replaced

180 Urinals

399 water closets

Replaced liquefied petroleum gas (LPG)-fired water heater with new technology heat pump for centralized hot water supply

50% reduction in consumption of LPG in ADB headquarters

*LPG was previously used to supply hot water to gyms, lockers, and kitchens.

Curbing Greenhouse Gas Emissions

ADB has gradually decreased its direct greenhouse gas (GHG) emissions. Today, all of ADB's electricity comes from 100% renewable sources—solar and geothermal. To reduce GHG emissions from business travel, ADB staff are asked to combine mission trips to minimize distances, seek out energy-efficient airlines, and maximize use of videoconferencing. Since 2016, we have offset our GHG emissions by purchasing voluntary emission certificates from ADB-supported renewable energy projects. *(GRI Disclosure 305, 305-1, 305-2, and 305-3)*

Practicing Water Efficiency

ADB uses water at our headquarters in various ways, ranging from watering plants, cooling, and cleaning of facilities, to food preparation, personal hygiene, and sanitation in restrooms and showers. Driven by the ADB mandate for green growth, we aimed to reduce water consumption at our headquarters by 3% per year in 2018 and 1% per year in 2019. In 2018, we reduced potable water consumption in our headquarters by 29%, exceeding our 3% target. *(GRI Disclosure 303-3)*

Figure 6: Water Conservation Performance, 2015–2019 (gallons)

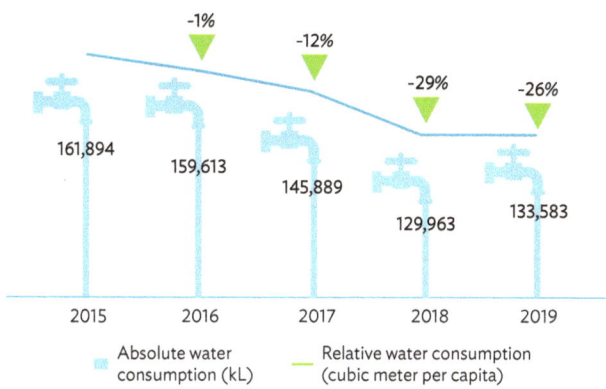

	2015	2016	2017	2018	2019
		-1%	-12%	-29%	-26%
Absolute water consumption	161,894	159,613	145,889	129,963	133,583

Absolute water consumption (kL)
Relative water consumption (cubic meter per capita)

kL = kiloliter
Note: % relative water consumption reduction vs. 2015

Figure 7: Total Recycled and Reused Water, 2017–2019 (m³)

	2017	2018	2019
Wastewater	9,483.00	8,894.60	6,715.00
Collected rainwater	2,441.00	3,063.00	5,659.00
Backwash water*	402.81	207.50	138.12
	12,326.81	12,165.10	12,512.12

m³ = cubic meter.
Note: % relative water consumption reduction vs. 2015.
* Backwash water: Water coming from cleaning of centralized water filtration tanks.

Table 2: Greenhouse Gas Intensity per Capita for ADB Headquarters, 2017–2019

	2017	2018	2019[a]
Total GHG emissions scopes 1, 2, and 3 (tons CO_2-equivalent)	11,334.39	11,680.98	12,349.22
Building occupancy[b] (persons)	6,144.00	6,617.00	6,804.00
GHG emissions intensity per capita	1.84	1.77	1.81

CO_2 = carbon dioxide, GHG = greenhouse gas.
[a] Indicative, subject to third-party verification.
[b] Building occupancy is based on an estimate by ADB's Office of Administrative Services of staff, consultants, contractors, service providers, and non-ADB personnel who are based at the ADB headquarters.

Figure 8: Total Water Withdrawn, 2017–2019 (m³)

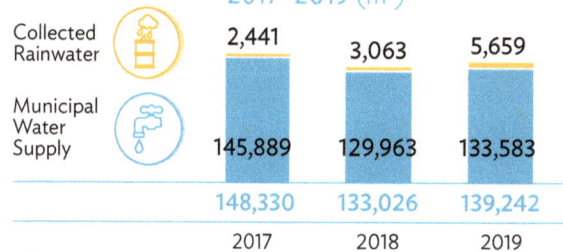

	2017	2018	2019
Collected Rainwater	2,441	3,063	5,659
Municipal Water Supply	145,889	129,963	133,583
	148,330	133,026	139,242

m³ = cubic meter.

Managing Our Energy

ADB's energy management capability continues to grow. Our ISO certifications not only call us to reduce the impact of our energy use on the environment, but also commit us to establish strategies and processes to increase energy efficiency and improve performance. From energy conservation programs (e.g., optimizing the use of our lighting and cooling systems) to raising staff awareness through events like Sustainability in Action, ADB strives to celebrate, support, and sustain the integrity of our environment.

Figure 9: Total Energy Consumption (MJ)

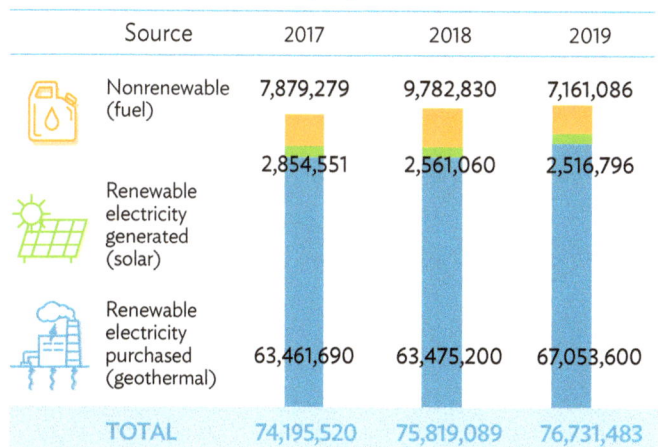

Source	2017	2018	2019
Nonrenewable (fuel)	7,879,279	9,782,830	7,161,086
Renewable electricity generated (solar)	2,854,551	2,561,060	2,516,796
Renewable electricity purchased (geothermal)	63,461,690	63,475,200	67,053,600
TOTAL	74,195,520	75,819,089	76,731,483

MJ = megajoules.

Table 3: Energy Intensity, 2017–2019

	2017	2018	2019
Total Energy consumption (MJ)	74,195,520	75,819,089	76,731,483
Floor area (m²)	144,025	147,092	153,146
Energy Intensity (MJ per m²)	515	515	501

MJ = megajoules, m² = square meter.

Figure 10: Electricity Performance, 2015–2019

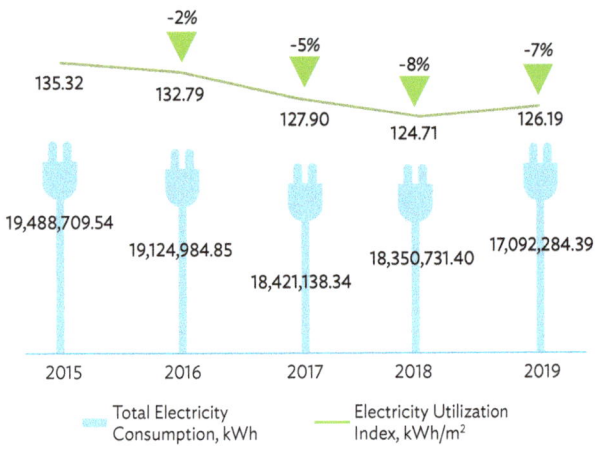

	2015	2016	2017	2018	2019
Electricity Utilization Index	135.32	132.79 (-2%)	127.90 (-5%)	124.71 (-8%)	126.19 (-7%)
Total Electricity Consumption, kWh	19,488,709.54	19,124,984.85	18,421,138.34	18,350,731.40	17,092,284.39

■ Total Electricity Consumption, kWh
— Electricity Utilization Index, kWh/m²

kWh = kilowatt-hour, kWh/m² = kilowatt-hour per square meter.
Note: % change in Electricity Utilization Index vs. 2015.

Promoting Knowledge on Green Building Practices

Through Sustainability Tours of our headquarters and facilities, participants from ADB, universities, private organizations, and local and international communities learn about conserving energy, water, and managing waste.

2018
22 sessions

2019
16 sessions

Sustainability in Action Week

Information and education campaigns raise awareness within the ADB community about sustainability and conservation practices. These awareness campaigns happen alongside World Environment Day and World Oceans Day.

Figure 11: ADB's 10-Point Sustainability in Action Plan

ADB Sustainability in Action
10 ways to walk the talk

Lower CO₂ emissions for missions
Use video conferencing when possible, bundle your missions, and choose the most direct route.

Turn it off
Turn off your lights, lamp and computer when you leave the office.

Take the stairs
Use the stairs instead of using the elevator.

Save water
Report leaks. Minimize water use.

Bring your mug
Use a mug or glass for beverages. Refuse plastic bottles. Refuse plastic straws.

Conserve paper
Use electronic copies for documents. Print back-to-back using recycled paper.

Segregate waste
Segregate your waste so it can be disposed of properly.

Consume what you need
Buy only what you need and use less.

Open your blinds
Use less energy by using natural lighting.

Commute sustainably
Bike or walk to work if you can. Carpool. Use public transport. Use a vehicle with low emissions.

OAS@Work
Passion to excel. Committed to deliver.

CO₂ = carbon dioxide.

Saving Materials and Resources

Organizations like ADB use large quantities of materials and resources during construction and operation, which generate waste. Managing resource procurement and reducing waste is integral to our green agenda. From sourcing building materials and administrative goods and services locally to reducing paper and single-use plastics in our headquarters, ADB continually strives to reduce consumption and waste and lessen our footprint.

Figure 12: Paper Consumption Monitoring per Year, 2015 Baseline

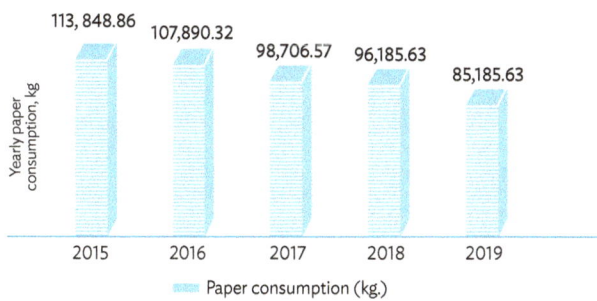

- 2015: 113, 848.86
- 2016: 107,890.32
- 2017: 98,706.57
- 2018: 96,185.63
- 2019: 85,185.63

Yearly paper consumption, kg

Paper consumption (kg.)

kg = kilogram.

Reducing ADB's Plastic Footprint

In 2018 and 2019, ADB embarked on a mission to significantly reduce single-use, nonrecyclable plastic across our entire food services operations (i.e., ADB headquarters and all internal events). We met with level service staff, concessionaires, and suppliers on plans and initiatives to phase out single-use plastic wherever feasible. We started with eliminating plastic straws, lids, and utensils. Our cafeteria and subconcessionaire stalls stopped offering water and beverages in plastic bottles and food wrapped in plastic film. Concessionaire stalls transitioned to glass bottles, chopsticks wrapped in paper, and reusable and/or biodegradable or paper takeaway containers. Simultaneously, we launched a sustained Information Education and Communications Campaign for ADB personnel and all visitors.

Table 4: Plastics in Kitchen and Dining Average % Reduction

Baseline 14–18 May 2018		Average % reduction	
		2018	2019
Bags (pcs)	338	72%	97%
Packaging (pcs)	2,803	77%	91%
Butter and jam container (pcs)	479	91%	100%
Wrap (g)	36,762	22%	51%
PET bottles (pcs)	894	88%	94%
Cups and lids (pcs)	1,194	67%	88%
Straws (pcs)	164	89%	100%
Chopsticks (pcs)	601	70%	100%

g = gram, pcs. = pieces, PET = polyethylene terephthalate.

Table 5: Plastics in Beverage Stalls Typical % Reduction

Baseline 14–18 May 2018 (pcs)		Typical % reduction	
		2018	2019
Straws	1,317	92%	96%
Cups and lids	3,736	78%	79%
Utensils	131	37%	69%
PET bottles	730	86%	87%

pcs. = pieces.

Table 6: Plastics in Stewarding Typical % Reduction

Baseline 14–18 May 2018		Typical % reduction	
		2018	2019
Plastic Bag (g)	9,400	74%	73%

g = gram.

Asian Development Bank Sustainability Report 2020
Part I: Highlights

The *Asian Development Bank Sustainability Report* has been produced biennially since 2007. It enables stakeholders to understand and assess ADB's sustainability performance in its project investments, technical assistance, knowledge services, and corporate footprint. The report consists of two parts. Part I: Highlights presents the major economic, social, and environmental impacts of ADB's operations and headquarters for 2018 and 2019. Part II: The Global Reporting Initiative Content Index provides detailed information and data on the integration of sustainability in ADB's operations, facilities, and organizational activities against the reporting standards of the Global Reporting Initiative.

About the Asian Development Bank

ADB is committed to achieving a prosperous, inclusive, resilient, and sustainable Asia and the Pacific, while sustaining its efforts to eradicate extreme poverty. Established in 1966, it is owned by 68 members —49 from the region. Its main instruments for helping its developing member countries are policy dialogue, loans, equity investments, guarantees, grants, and technical assistance.

ISBN 978-92-9262-718-8

ASIAN DEVELOPMENT BANK
6 ADB Avenue, Mandaluyong City
1550 Metro Manila, Philippines
www.adb.org